# How to Build a TANF Program Welfare to Work Program and Rebuild America's Inner City Urban Communities?

I0481511

By Eddie Franklin

I dedicate this with grateful thanks to Eric Lofholm, for his encouragement and offering his training programs on closing, especially the program of writing a book in a day which took last year and now I am finally finishing my first book.

I also want to thank him for his book "Step into Your Vision Top Business Leaders Share Their Goals Setting Secrets" by Sharmayah Sarrucco and Eric Lofhom which I have read three times and am reading it again. I have written on the subject of time management but found new simple relations in this book.

I have read Napoleon Hill's book
"Think and Grow Rich"
five times, looking for the secret mentioned in the preface and in every chapter of the book, I finally found it. It was simply to make a decision and the universe/God would provide the means and people to make that decision happen.

The Book "Step into Your Vision Top Business Leaders Share Their Goals Setting Secrets" makes it even simpler, that is to set goals, WRITE THEM DOWN and read them every day and let your mind open at the unconscious level in order to change your mind.

All of the writers of this book state one simple principle that is encompassed in the act of establishing your goals to change your mind, thinking and to establish your intent and vision in your mind and you will get into action. Thank you again.

Eddie

# Table of Contents

## Chapter-1: Determine Your Why

Why do you want to create Welfare to Work Program? I want to create one because I fell strongly for the building up the housing stock in the inner cities. My first exposure with building was in my childhood while living at my grandfather's farm in Mississippi. I saw my parents build their own from scratch on the farm, and then later when I was 8 or 9 years old, I was asked, asked is a mild word for how we started to help build a house. A man named Mr. Coleman, who lived in Hopkins Park Illinois in Pembroke Township, in the dead of winter and framing for the roof as the foundation had already been poured in concrete, later after 2 years the house was finished and it still stands today.

You have to ask yourself who will benefit from such a program in your community.

What are some of the outcomes that you see coming from such a program for other people and for yourself and your community and outcomes for society at large? I will attempt to answer some of these questions for myself and the communities of Chicago Illinois. The program can and should be implemented in every major urban community in America where unemployment is high and there is a high rate of crime and criminal backgrounds of men and women for largely non-violent crimes such as selling cigarettes or Marijuana which has been found to have medical benefits and is being legalized in many states including Illinois, which approved the license of growing of marijuana for medical purposes and a large number who are on some

1

type of public assistance, as these are federal in their origin and is available in every State in some form or another.

In addition to all the altruistic reasons I am developing this type of program to attract investors to the program and build a multi-billion dollar business operating in every State and to personally become wealthy.
There won't be only an economic benefit but investors will be benefitted personally, spiritually and emotionally, to feel good and joyful.

## Chapter-2: What is The Welfare to Work Program or TANAF (Temporary Assistance to Needy Families)?

Who among us has not had some need of assistance at some time in our lives, either economic or spiritual?

It is a program where men have to be married and living with their wives and women have to be pregnant and everyone under 50 years of age has to submit a social responsibility plan that is approved by a caseworker. The program has been largely forgotten but it was a part of Bill Clintons 1996.

Economic Recovery and Social Responsibility Act of 1996 states that it requires that a person must work 20 hours per month in order to gain benefits of medical care and food stamps or SNAP.

Why is it Important to move people From Welfare to Work?
Talking about the spiritual level first, it gives a person a sense of self-worth, makes them feel they are a positive contributing member of society, a father, a mother, a provider for their children and community and a role model of how life should be lived.
This provides exposure in the workplace and an opportunity to gain marketable skills and an income, in order to provide for them.
This also ensures a retirement income through Social Security if nothing else.

It assures that Social Security does not go bankrupt and will be available for us and them. I am Baby Boomer of 71 years old and figures show that 10,000 of us are retiring and collecting Social Security every week and leaving the workforce.

We are living longer than average age of a male, which is from 69 to 72 years and for a female which is from 70 to 83 years. This is a matter of enlightened self-interest for me. However, I am not totally counting on Social Security for my income however; having it does increase the quality of my retirement.

Figures from a recent newspaper article show the effective workforce are the lowest since 1972 and another article says that the technology revolution is having a devastating effect on job lost in China. The long-sought market for outsourcing of manufacturing, the information age has had a tremendous effect on job lost in America where jobs such as customer support and other functions have been outsourced to English speaking such as India. The GIG economy has taken root and it's hard to find, even clerical work. There are jobs in the hidden economy and they do not pay into America's social security system.

**Chapter-3: How to Get Use of This Subsided Labor?**

How Can You Get uses of these 20 hours per month and how can you use this subsidized labor. Many states allow getting trainees directly from the Department of Human Services and a few have used some of the money from the federal government to give grants under RFP request for Proposals and have awarded grant money to many non-profit and -profit organizations to provide training and certificate programs for individuals enrolled in these programs for all manner of training, but none of them provide in one area as I know of and that is Internet marketing.

These type of jobs can't be easily outsourced overseas. Why internet marketing? Most of these people have no idea that they can make a living as an affiliate marketer for someone else's products on sites such as Click Bank and Amazon. The advent of the information age will create the greatest transference of wealth in American history, certainly since the invention of the personal computer.

Moore's Law is moving at a rate that it was never intended to, accelerating computing and reducing the cost as never before says Raymond Kurzweil in his book "The Singularity is Near When Humans Transcend Biology". It is more cost-effective than ever before to start a home business, with the use of Facebook, Instagram, and LinkedIn, but not many of these grantees are focusing on this opportunity for self-employment.

I was at seminar presented by Facebook, The Chicago Women's Development Center and congresswoman Robin Kelly of the 2nd congressional district of Illinois and SCORE (Service Core of Retired Executives) which I was formerly a member of, it was held at the new Harbor View International Golf course on the Southside of the city of Chicago in the Roseland community which is 90% black. Over 400 people attended yet only less than 20 minorities/black were in attendance, most of the attendees were white women running online businesses with gross receipts of over $50,000 dollars per year. Congresswoman stated that the implementation of the goal for women-owned businesses of 5%, some 40 years ago for federal contracts the recently reported she said that women-owned businesses had dropped to 2% mark.

Though I am an internet net marker and Life Coach but for sake of this book I am focusing on some business that can't be totally transferred overseas and that is housing here in America.

There are grantees that spend over $50,000,000 million dollars in Illinois, along providing training for 8 to 10 weeks in specific skills in the building trades such as setting a toilet, hanging a door or piece of drywall but none of them provide a job. These are the perfect skills for a rehabber or handyman, which do not require formal certification from some building trade union. These skills are sourly needed in America. In early 60s in Chicago, the city college lost the programs provided by

17 union apprentice training programs, which were held at Washburn Trade School and unions slowly started to move the HUB of all of this training to Elk Grove Village, which was 40 to 50 miles outside the city of Chicago, where minorities did not have transportation to get to classes. This similar thing happened nationwide and there is a shortage of Americas skilled tradesmen and women at an astounding rate and many of the jobs nationwide are being held by undocumented aliens.

**Chapter-4: What happened to Washburn Trade School in Chicago?**

From Wikipedia
The overturn of Plessy verse Ferguson marked the down fall of Washburn Trade School as part of the Chicago public schools Plessy v. Ferguson, 163 US 537 (1896) was a landmark constitutional law case of the US Supreme Court decided in 1896. It upheld state racial segregation laws for public facilities under the doctrine of "separate but equal".[1] The decision was handed down by a vote of 7 to 1 with the majority opinion written by Justice Henry Billings Brown and the dissent written by Justice John Marshall Harlan.

"Separate but equal" remained standard doctrine in U.S. law until its repudiation in the 1954 Supreme Court decision Brown v. Board of Education.[2]

Washburn handled all of the vocational apprenticeships within the Chicago Public Schools. However, problems began to arise. Prior to the mid to late 1960s, the school was primarily white. When the school began to be desegregated, unions began to pull programs. There were 17 different unions at the school in 1965. A mere 13 years later, the number of unions had been cut to nearly half, with 8 remaining. By the time of the school's first closure in 1993, only 2 programs were remaining.

From the 60s to the 90s, unions began to pull their support and pull their programs out of the school. By 1993, only the culinary program remained, and after that it moved to Kennedy-King CC. In 1996, the school got closed. It was left to decay until demolition several years ago.

From Wikipedia
This left the city college system with only basic certificate programs which were offered in just trades mostly at the Dawson Technology Institute. This is little more than what the awardees are providing under the grants from the Department of Human Services, and not sufficient for entry into union apprenticeship program that qualifies members for union membership.

This move was to limit the access of minorities to trades training; now the chickens have come home to Russ in the shortage of qualified workers and the retirement of workers. A token has been granted some 30 years later at Kennedy King College where there is some skills trades training but the many foci in the culinary arts for the hospitality industry thus keeping minorities in the Aunt Jama Uncle Ben syndrome of the one who cooks your food, and or to be the butlers for the downtown hotel.

This is a tremendous opportunity for anyone in this digital age. Even during slavery blacks were allowed to become tradesmen, though their labor was farmed out and the salary was paid to their owners. Jobs in the building trades have hourly salaries of up $40 or $60 dollars per hour and more.
Set your own goals as to how to use this program, these 20 hours of subsidized labor.

## Chapter-5: Why I Chose Real Estate Rehabbing of Housing.

In the next few pages I will answer the 5 questions of WHY, WHO WHEN, Where, HOW I have chosen rehab of homes due to the need for returning homes that are abandoned and/or in need of repair in our communities to the highest and best use and need to provide the meaningful stainable jobs in our communities, and this will stabilize the urban flight and the decreasing of the tax base in many inner-city communities and the need for individuals with skills to make these type of repairs in carpentry, plumbing and electrical. I am talking about skills, not some formal union certificate which these men and women have denied.

WHY?
My experience as a management consultant at a major international management consulting company, which I started working in the field over 40 years ago, and my experience as a management consultant for
disadvantage businesses working under a grant from the US Department of Commerce in the minority business development agency and also my experience as a superintendent for both the Chicago Housing Authority, and The Chicago Park District supervising men and women in all of the building trades, and finally the ownership of my own construction company.

WHEN?

Last year I developed a written plan for the implementation of this program and started to develop the resources and relationships to make it happen. The goals are measurable and attainable with specific outcomes and the time frame for accomplishing them. They are included in the last part of this book.

WHO?

You must build a team of people by attracting the people who will make you achieve your goals, by holding you accountable.

There are several categories of non-profits organizations you should include. First you should include both nonprofit and for profit that has been successful in gaining grants from your department of Human services to provide training to individuals who are enrolled in the program, particularly those that are training in the building trades in many States Including Illinois have given grants for this proposal, Illinois recently awarded over $50,000, 000 fifty million dollars a year for this purpose, by answering an RFP a request for proposal and being one of the grantee for these funds. These organizations provide 8 to 10 weeks training in a skill area and pay the individuals while they are getting their training. Once their training finishes, these organizations are more than willing to identify some of their best prospects for employment with your firm and they usually pay the graduates for the first 40 hours while they are your employees.

Look for organizations that teach GED literacy and computer skills, many of these are funded by the Dollar General Department Chains stores, contact them and find out who are the grantees in your area.

Look for organizations that address the need of ex-offender, the mass incarcerated which are over 2,000,000,000 according to Michelle Alexander in her book the NEW JIM CROW. Many of them were sentenced under the 3 sticks legislation for non-violent crimes.

Look for organizations that teach anger management as many of these individuals have these issues and have to take these courses to maintain the parole status and remain free.

Look for organizations that help ex-offenders acclimate to society by helping them with getting proper identification such as birth certificates, driver licenses, apply for benefits and to find housing.

Look for organizations that provide transitional housing for ex- offenders.

Check with your locals of the Urban League for any sources or information they can provide you with.

Check with the local offices of the SAFER Foundation, an organization funded very heavily to assist ex-offenders and they also provide training fund to ex-offenders.

Check with local Churches that may be involved and have a prison ministry.

Check with your local city and county government and see what they have to offer.

Check with for-profits firms in your area that might be able to help and if not start your own Limited. Liability Corporation LLC.
Start groups on FACEBOOK and LinkedIn and join groups that are aligned with your aims on these sites.
Start fan pages on Facebook and build your friends network. Even advertise on Facebook, it is very reasonable in cost and develop a profile on both of these sites and people with like interest will contact you.

Lenders will seek you out to provide private and hard money loans and other resources.
Establish a Go Fund Me Account and People will donate to your efforts.
Some will want to become employers to your trainees, and other may have funding resources you are not aware of.

Choose these relations carefully as you have always to maintain strict vertical and horizontal integrations of goals, particularly with non-profits and for-profit organizations as not create a conflict of interest and the problem of co-mingling of funds.


WHERE
This program can be implemented in any and every State in the United States since it is a federally mandated program. It should be implemented in any community where the real estate acquisition cost of a home is less than 20% of The ARV after repair value and

cost of repairs is less than 30% of the ARV after repair value in these communities, In 1984, I and the members of my family purchased 3 homes from the US Department of Housing and Urban Development (HUD), all for less than $10,000 Ten Thousand Dollars, these homes are valued at near $80,000 Eighty Thousand Dollars each today.

The Obama Library in Jackson Park in Chicago is seeing real estate prices rising at a tremendous rate, people will be coming to the area from all over the world and growth will be like that of the World Exposition for growth in some parts of Englewood And South Shore. Back in 1984, these homes had to be researched very well before we purchased them since the realtors assigned to weekly inspect these homes but rarely did their jobs. With the advent of the cell phone which takes pictures, these realtors can't simply go to the home once a month or never at all, they have to visit these weekly as required and take pictures which are time dated as to the condition of the homes. The results is many of these home require very little repair and are generally in good condition and have not changed much since the evicted tenant was foreclosed on.

The problem is that most lenders will not make loans to repair these home, particularly when Zillow and Redfin have labeled these as high crime killing zones. This has given way to hard money lending at high interest rates if it is available at all and the banks will not lend unless the home came pass FHA (Federal Housing Authority) guidelines. This has given way to a new type of hard money financing, that of equity financing in which many hard money lenders will lend up to 70% of the after repair value of a home or residential property for the acquisition and repairs. This allows them to take advantage of the tremendous loss in price of homes in many inner city communities, note I said price and not value, but they will usually only lend to a Corporation or Limited liability Corporation. I believe to avoid the homestead provisions provided to individual home owners of real estate law in many states in America. These loans are for investors with limited liability corporations and businesses only, so start one.

Contact me at
efranklin@coopcommuniytfanancing.com
for information on the best hard money lending sites.

BANKS
Choose a community that has strong community banks. Why community banks? The community bank have a vested interested in your community, you can establish a personal relationship with these types of banks and have access to the key decisions makers for getting loans. They also have knowledge of the community and potential beneficial changes that may be happening in your community. Many of these banks have first time home buyers programs where individuals have to go through training and are approved to purchase your newly rehabbed home and many States have Developmental Authorities that provide Grants for first

time home buyers. These grants can be up to 4% four percent of the purchase price of the home, which can be used as a down payment or to closing cost. In Illinois the IDA Illinois Development Authority is the grantor of these grants.

Chose an area where there is a strong demand for housing, areas with HUD section 8 housing is a candidate since many people on section 8 have jobs and in some states, section 8 will contribute to the mortgage payment.

Building per fab homes is an excellent opportunity. Look for areas with large numbers of vacant lots, the abandoned US Steel plant location in the South Chicago community has a plan for building prefab homes in Chicago.
This is an example: Under the Chicago 8080 Lakeshore Master Plan inspired by Barcelona's Mega Block.

Approach which plans to build 12,000 homes on this site in 4 phases The plan is to build a manufacturing plant on the site, this would provide economies of scale reduced transportation cost and be able to deliver per fab modest cost homes for as little as $70, Dollars per square foot. This means that a 1000 square foot 3-bedroom could be built for $70,000.
This would be a wonderful opportunity for profit in the Roseland Community where the average cost of a similar home is $125,000 one hundred and twenty five thousand dollars. It increased from $100,000 one

hundred thousand to $125,000 one hundred and twenty five dollars thousand dollars up (25%), and still increasing according to Zillow. Perhaps due the building of the new international golf course on land that is close to what was the city dump.

This land has closed for many years. Already South Shore Drive has been widened to two lanes and extended for 79th Street to Hammond Indiana. Prefab homes are built at the factory and are only assembled at the sites; this would minimize the need for plumbers, electricians and carpenters. It would be perfect for individuals with limited skills of only the assembly of homes. Developers are building $400,000 four hundred thousand dollar prefab homes on every vacant lot they can find. In certain communities on the North side of the city of Chicago, many older homes in certain communities are being demolished to make way for new construction.

The Cook County Land Development Authority (CCLDA), once a nonprofit is now a profit organization that has been given the authority to acquire vacant lots and many vacant homes in Cook County. They are eager to work with anyone to redevelop these lots and homes. Last quarter, they put out a call for anyone with information on multifamily vacant building in their area that they would be eager and more than able to go to court and take these buildings from the owners that are not paying the taxes or maintaining their property.

They have special programs and in some cases you are able to purchase a lot for $1 one dollar, if you live on the block where the lot is located and at reasonable rates to the general public. They are aggressively working to restore inner-city Cook County and this model is being adopted nationwide to return this land to the tax rolls.

## Chapter-6: RELEASED WITHOUT HOPE.

Remember according to Michelle Alexander in her bestselling book "The New Jim Crow", over 2,000,000 two million men and women incarcerated in American prisons, most of them for nonviolent crimes such as possession of or sale of marijuana, which is now according to many sources on the verge of becoming legalized in the United States. In the month of September it was legalized and licensed for growth and sale of it for medical purposes, in Illinois and nationwide, again remember that is no accident that these men and women are being released in droves to fill the declining labor force as baby boomer retires at a rate of 10,000 ten thousand per week.

They are being released after being in prison for fifteen to twenty years. Congressman of Chicago, Danny Davis recently stated on WKKC 89.5 FM Chicago', Kennedy King College radio station, that the congressional black caucus make a mistake of pushing for the 3 strikes, you're out prison legislation, that commended many young men and women to long-term prison sentence to feed the need for employment in rust belt communities where manufacturing jobs were lost, as the jobs were moved overseas or the South and South West parts of the country, where prisons have become the main employers in many of these communities, in the rust belt and our scared young men and women are the products produced.

They are being released with no place to go, no new way of thinking, no hope for a better life, and no hope for a retirement or social security since many of them are functionally illiterate and have never or very little worked on a job which paid into social security. Unless we give them some alternatives, the only option for them is to feign some form of physical or mental illness, which provides on the productive outcome to society or return to prison for committing some more serious crimes.

Insanity and insane thinking are being spread throughout the inner city communities across America; no wonder the murder rate is so high in these communities, not only in Chicago but in every community.

Where, there are abandoned homes on block after block. The problem that in Chicago is reported more perhaps as a left over for the Al Capone days of the Saint Valentine Massacre, but I am old enough to remember when Detroit Michigan, Gary Indiana, and even Little Rock Arkansas were the murder capitals of America, remember gang banging in Little Rock. Check it out on YouTube.

Thurgood Marshall the first black judge appointed to the supreme court of the United State said in the book by Carl T. Rowan Dream Makers, Dream Breakers "One of my great disillusionments was the delay of the government to implement the dictates of the 1954

Brown Versus the Board of Education decision". The government delayed any concern for education until Barbara Bush's program of one child left behind, two generations were lost in that period of more than 40 years. This is the generation we must reclaim from the prisons of the America's. America needs them now. When are we going to take control of the labor in our communities and use it for our own economic development, within those communities?

Knowledge is more powerful than authority. With the knowledge of how to do something, a person does not need the authority of being the journeymen tradesmen person in the building trades. They can make their own job in their own community.
 Knowledge is God-given while authority is a creation of man. What we want to give our young men and women is knowledge, since we have been denied authority in the building trades unions.

The whole history of western civilization has involved the direction of labor, from Abraham, David, Solomon to the slave trade, to the civil war which freed black labor from the agrarian south to work in the industrial north.

Who can accuse us of directing this labor force in helping us building a successful real estate and construction business, as we help rebuild our communities while giving them training and life skills to make a living in society at large, certainly not God him or herself.

Raymond Kruzwield the founder of the singularity movement and sited by some as one of the three most influential men in America at the University of Chicago in his book "The Singularity is Near When Humans Transcend Biology" lobbied for a new course of study to be introduced at high schools in Chicago and nationwide, where students would take a 6 year program which included a heavy dose of technology and after they graduate they would have a job waiting for them at one of the high tech companies. This is coming to reality for the present generation of youth, with the new high schools and new programs.

The Major of Chicago Rob Emmanuel announced on October the 10th 2017, that a similar program was being introduced to Chicago schools. This is wonderful for the current high school students, but what about their parents, the generation from 25 to 50 years old? This is the group I am concerned about.

## Chapter-7: Our Business Model.

We will focus on working with the realtors that specialize in foreclosed homes. This represents only about 20% twenty per cent of the realtors in a given market. These realtors will have 80% eighty per cent of all the foreclosures in that market. We will look for HUDs from, the US Housing and Urban Development, Fannie May, Freddie Mac and bank foreclosures. Wholesalers of homes that get them under contract and will assign their contracts to us for a fee that are not in the business of fix and flip or may have some that they want to assign, and of course homes from private sellers.

We will focus on lean Rehabbing while providing quality homes for your communities at a cost that is affordable for the incomes that are available in those communities. Our administrative staff will be no more than 2 people, they will be cross-trained all of the functions listed above, our trades' people will never exceed 30 to start and they will be given full-time employment and they too will be cross-trained. As much as possible, remember that we are not talking about union trained people. This will be at the height of our production of 303 homes per year. The staffing will start at 2 in field administration, 4 in skills trades and 2 in office administration that will later be increased proportionally as required. This is for the first year, production of 60 homes. The average salary will be about $40,000 for trades person plus benefits and $25,000 year for administration personnel and 2 foremen after 6 months of first year at $50,000 year, but only one in the first 2.5 years, the second in the second half of the 5-year plan. We are not talking about 4 years' apprentice programs.

America is in need of an effective labor force. It is no act of benevolence that men and women are being released from prisons who were convicted under the 3 strikes law for nonviolent crimes.

  Being released to work at McDonalds or Ford Motor company for $15 fifteen dollars an hour, when I worked in the auto industry as a foreman over 48 years ago the salaries of my pressman was over $60,000 sixty thousand dollars per year without over time.

Construction is the only part of real estate that's measured by GDP. It affects many other areas of the economic that aren't measured as well. For example, a decline in real estate sales eventually leads to a decline in real estate prices. This lowers the value of all homes, whether owners are actively selling it or not. It reduces the number of home equity loans available to owners. They will cut back on consumer spending. Real Estate prices are lower now than they were in 1984. The value of residential real estate has been decreased by at least 30%. One 4-bedroom, 4 car garage, 3.5 baths, 4800 square feet home at 801 East Oakwood Blvd in Chicago's, Bronzes Ville community had a value of $1.200.000 in 2005, this home had its value decreased to $450,000 in 2010, it recently was sold for $745, 000.

Now is the time to get in the market again. Zillow's forecast for this house is that it will return to over a million dollars in the next 5 years, when the river rises, all boats rise, even those at the lower end of the market that we target.

Nearly 70% of the U.S. economy is based on personal consumption. A reduction in consumer spending contributes to a downward spiral in the economy. That leads to further unemployment, further reduction in income, and further reduction in consumer spending.

A baby boom economy is not sustainable; we must reach back for the lost generation who are aged 25 to 50 years old.

This is the age group of which many has never or worked very little under a social security plan. They find themselves looking forward to 69 with little of any type of income to sustain them. Again, I say, therefore with no hope, they will chose to fake some type of physical or mental illness in order to claim a SSI disability check. What alternative has America given this lost generation except to fake some type of illness? This program can offer a solution. If a person thinks or plays that they are crazy longer enough, God will give them up to a retro bate mind and they might feel justified in killing someone, or go back to prison, who in these communities does not know someone who is on some form of disability, I have known many of them when my family and I managed 14 fourteen units of SRO single room occupancy housing, whose only goal in life was to accomplish this, perhaps even someone in their own families. This has been a life's goal for many.

This is not to say that there are not some that are ill and in need of this type of support.

**Chapter-8: Strategic Plan.**

Our strategic plan is to mobilize America's inner city communities by institutionalizing, our model, The Chicago Model and driving the housing recovery to our communities, by establishing coalitions nationwide.

You may ask if this recovery has been going since 2015 and the Dodd-Frank has not been amended yet. What is going on? We have not seen any recovery in our communities. There is a principle in economics called the Perfect Market Theory which says, that all information that is available is known and the market has already adjusted to that information. This means that as soon as the platforms of the two parties were known and they both supported the amending of Dodd-Frank to something closer to Glass-Stegall, the banks started to lend beyond their reserve requirements, but not in our communities.

   We must drive recovery to our communities, here I do not mean like driving a car. This is the analogy, growing up in Mississippi on my grandfather's farm where we had two Missouri mules, the big mule Trump and a smaller one. A spring morning my father took me out to harness the mules and the first thing he did was that he took a singletree and hit big Trump in the head. I asked my daddy why you hit Trump in the head. He smiled and said "I had to get his attention". This is what we have to do to big Trump of the banking industry, get their attention by massive media campaigns centered on YouTube, and Google AdWords blogs which are both

Advertising means and income streams. We will get paid for every view of our video on YouTube and every click on our monetized blog. We will establish a Leverage/multiplier which means that once you do it and post it, it keeps on giving results, like the above mentioned, the Amazon Channel, podcasts, Facebook Groups, LinkedIn Groups, and Publishing a book.

The first thing we must do is to get someone from welfare to work that is willing, concerned and want to work to restore our communities. We must harness/horse collar the banks to do work for and with our communities.

Definition from Wikipedia
"A singletree is a piece of wood about 3 feet long wrapped with iron used to hook horse or mule to a wagon or plow to do work."
The action of a singletree is to balance the pull from alternate shoulders as the animal walks. It is used especially when the animal is in a breast collar harness because this can easily rub the shoulders if the pull is uneven. It is needed less for an animal in a horse collar, as the pull does not pass over the shoulders in the same way.
The only way to modify the behavior of a person or a company is confrontation and there are many styles of confrontation, one is the implied threat. We must create

the implied threat by publishing on webinars, on YouTube, on Facebook, in blogs and by writing books of success stories and conditions that need to be changed and that have changed.

All over the internet to men and women are establishing authorities by supplying content that the internet is hungry for, we can become authorities in our own niches as they relate to our common concerns.

## Chapter-9: The Goals and Objectives.

I believe that it's fairly easy to establish a statically correlation between the numbers of vacant and boarded up homes on a block in a neighborhood and rate of murders and shooting. The more the abandoned buildings, the more is the loss of self-respect and dignity resulting in more killings. There have been reported 750 murders in Chicago, Illinois last year, in 2016.

From The Southside Weekly Magazine
"While there were fewer foreclosures in Chicago in the first half of 2014 than the first half of 2013 that has not signaled a recovery citywide. The homes made vacant by the housing crisis, like 1474 West 73rd, are now themselves the cause of what experts call "negative spillover effects," and the people who live in the most affected neighborhoods continue to suffer from them. A single foreclosed, tax delinquent and vacant home can lower the value of neighboring homes by as much as ten percent, according to a working paper from the Federal Reserve Bank of Cleveland. Many blocks in neighborhoods on the South Side have more than one such home. In Englewood, 11.1% of residences had been vacant for more than two years as of the first quarter of 2014—up from 8.1% in 2010—according to data from the Institute of Housing Studies (IHS) at DePaul. This was the second highest among community areas in the city, after Riverdale. 8.3% had been vacant for more than two years in West Englewood (up from 5.4% in 2010), and 7.6% had been vacant for the same period in nearby

Woodlawn (up from 4.6% in 2010). Homes that have been vacant for more than two years are often unmaintained and have the worst effects on surrounding property values, although other vacancies, which the IHS does not collect data for, are harmful as well.

 "Most of the vacancies *in Woodlawn+ are because of the predatory lending stuff and people losing their homes through foreclosure," says Butler.

 The housing crisis first hit homeowners directly through subprime loans. Around the country, subprime loans with high-interest rates were disproportionately sold to people in poor, minority communities. At the peak of the housing crisis, almost half of all loans sold to African-Americans were subprime, the Center for Responsible Lending, a research nonprofit, found. Court affidavits reveal that Wells Fargo loan officers called their black customers "mud people," and the subprime loans they sold them "ghetto loans." In 2007, Wells Fargo sold black homeowners in the Chicago area the highest-priced loans of any of the nation's top ten lenders, according to the Chicago Reporter. (Many of the vacancies the Weekly found with unrecorded deeds also belonged to Wells Fargo.)

 But even those residents who managed to stay afloat on their loans continue to struggle with a problem they didn't create—the vacant properties around them. As banks take over homes in foreclosure, but don't file the deeds and don't maintain the properties, they continue to exacerbate this problem.

In July 2011, the city passed updated regulations for vacant buildings, instituting the requirement that all vacant residential buildings be registered with the Department of Buildings and tasking mortgage holders with maintenance of properties within thirty days of their owners having vacated them. The ordinance extended the definition of property ownership in Chicago to include mortgage lenders, and required them to take responsibility for the buildings abandoned by those whose mortgages they'd serviced. This was in part an effort to cut down on the number of zombie properties, cracking down on those who would let vacant properties sit in limbo.

The ordinance passed unanimously in City Council and earned praise from Mayor Rahm Emanuel but questions surrounded the legality of making the mortgage holders the owners of the homes.

"You can't just make a secured lender an owner because there's a word changed in the law," Linda Koch, president and CEO of the Illinois Bankers Association, a lobbying group, told the Huffington Post after the bill's passage.

"The only way that we are and should be responsible is if we are the actual owner and have the title to the property."

So, the law was amended that December—after negotiations with Bank of America, Wells Fargo, JPMorgan Chase, and PNC Bank—to make mortgage holders responsible for maintenance without legally considering them the owners until the foreclosure was completed.

In the second quarter of 2014, there were 33,073 homes in Chicago that had been vacant for over two years, according to an analysis of USPS/HUD vacancy data by the Institute for Housing Studies at DePaul. Only 18,718 vacant homes were registered with the city as of March.

Even among those properties that are registered as vacant with the city, many, if not most, have unpaid fines. 5915 South Ada, 658 West 62nd, and 6422 South Green are among them. Then there are even stranger cases, like that of 5734 South May. Though the house has been registered with the Buildings Department since last June under Wells Fargo (Wells Fargo still isn't on the deed) and has no unpaid fines, its windows are no longer boarded and secure—although they were when photos were taken for the city's registry—and it was slapped with a "First Time Vacant" notice on March 2.

"Most of the vacant buildings aren't registered *in accordance with the ordinance+ and paying, and they're not properly secured," says Cathy Gerlach, who directs the city's Micro-Market Recovery Program (MMRP), a program working to revitalize thirteen small, distressed areas of the city. The MMRP partners with community organizations in neighborhoods like Woodlawn and Englewood to reoccupy vacant buildings and keep people in their homes.

Not only do we have a situation where no one can buy it, but the new owner, which is the bank, isn't doing what they're supposed to," Gerlach says.

Spencer Cowan, head of research at the Woodstock Institute, a nonprofit housing research organization, says he started to notice the problem when preparing a recent report on zombie properties.

"*The banks+ had the title for a considerable amount of time before they took the deed to record," Cowan says. "It was obvious from that that there were instances where the bank got the title but didn't report it promptly." Cowan found that some banks were waiting to record the deeds until right before they could sell the properties off.

The Woodstock report on zombie properties, which focused only on those that never finished foreclosure or were still in foreclosure, was released in January 2014. Cowan doesn't consider properties that go through foreclosure with unrecorded deeds "zombies."
"You've got a party that is effectively unmarketable" he says, "but *the bank+ knows at some point the value of

that property is going to matter to it, so it has an interest in keeping the property up." "Banks that have not properly filed the recording of deeds on foreclosed properties occasionally present obstacles to the City's Law Department for code enforcement matters as well as for rehabbers," said John Holden, speaking on behalf of the City and the Law Department.

"This is happening all across urban America," he says. "Look at New Orleans." He then mentions the area south of Garfield and around Normal, where land has been purchased to expand the Norfolk Southern Railway. He says there will be other local developments that displace African-American people before transitioning to talk about how there's now a New Balance store on 55th Street in Hyde Park Real estate that plays an integral role in the U.S. economy. Residential real estate provides housing for families. It's often the greatest source of wealth and savings for many of them. Commercial real estate, which includes apartment buildings, creates spaces for jobs in retail, offices and manufacturing. Real estate income provides a source of revenue for millions.

By Kimberly Amadeo
In 2015, real estate construction contributed $990 billion to the nation's economic output.
That's 6% of U.S. Gross Domestic Product (GDP). That's getting closer to its peak of $1.195 trillion in 2006. At that time, it was a hefty 8.9% component of GDP. Real estate construction is labor intensive. That's why a drop-

in housing construction was a big contribution to the recession's high unemployment rate.

Construction is the only part of real estate that's measured by GDP. It affects many other areas of economic well-being that aren't measured as well. For example, a decline in real estate sales eventually leads to a decline in real estate prices. That lowers the value of all homes, whether owners are actively selling it or not. It reduces the number of home equity loans available to owners. They will cut back on consumer spending.

The article above from the Southside new letter only sees part of the problem but inherent in, the problem is and opportunity, the solution. Many people see the failure of the banks to record the deeds as a tactic to avoid responsibility for properties and avoiding taxes. Any good tax accountant can write off taxes and fines and take depreciation on the property and create a positive cash flow from the effort, but there is a more compelling reason the banks do not want to record the deeds and that is the reserves requirements set up under Dodd-Frank, which requires a bank to hold 10 % reserves for all its assets both conforming and non-conforming.  These nonconforming assets have an assessed value and 10% of that value must be held in reserves. This reduces the amount of money a bank can lend and make money off interest rate charges. The banks have already written off the loss on their taxes. Why would we expect that they put them back on their books or social responsibility, without some change in the reserve requirements? When have the banks been socially responsible to the black inner city communities? I see the opportunity inherent in changes in Dodd-Frank that would have reserve requirement more like Glass-Stegall, the 1933 Act that required banks to maintain a reserve of only 3%, both political parties and the new president support this move. This would possibly release 7% of the total assets in US Banks that are $13,000,000,000,000 Thirteen Trillion dollars or $910,000,000,000 Nineteen billion dollars for banks to lend. This would be mostly for home loans guaranteed by FHA loans. I believe we stand on the edge of one of the greatest economy recovery in the history of the American Housing Industry, look at the figures of 2015 in the article gained from a simple Google search By Kimberly Amadeo.

Churches in the vicinity of these properties should be our strongest alliances partners. There is a church and there is one on almost every corner in most of these communities. Interview people in the community on how long has a property been vacant, and what they think the effect has been in the community and what they think needs to be done to correct the situation, while we video tape for YouTube. This would be the first wave of videos to be published. We must harness the power of the local Churches in the affected areas.

We do not need their money, we need their names. The goal would be to get the banks to work with us to solve the problem of vacant and abandoned building in our communities, here in Chicago.

Many organizations fail due of improper integration of goals, acquisition against sales and operations i.e. sales marketing and rehab. We must vertical and horizontal integrate our real estate businesses fix and flip, buy and hold, and lease option with our welfare to work skills training program, and prison ministries program. We must always make sure that the goals of these functional areas intersect at the proper level at all times, that is why I believe that the organismic Z Theory is better that the mechanistic X or Y Theories. The mechanistic approach is too static with not enough feedback for an effective and optimized profitable organization. The skills levels of the trainees must always match the level of training needed for a profitable rehab and resell. The acquisition cost must always match the market demand, as the skills level Increase, the more complex and costly the project is that we can undertake.

http://www.businessballs.com/mcgregor.htm

Introduced by Douglas McGregor in the 50s, but there is another theory the Z theory which blurs the lines between functional areas, where everyone shares their strengths and over laps into the other areas when the opportunity presents itself. This theory does not strive for perfection but for continuous improvement.

The theory was introduced by Dr. Ken Ouchi which promotes the sharing of skills in small groups, and it increases the loyalty of the members as no one is the King, in any domain but all share ideas to improve the

Productivity of the organization. The book is called Z-Theory by Dr. Ken Ouchi and can be purchased on Amazon. We want to build long time investors relations. https://en.wikipedia.org/wiki/Theory_Z_of_Ouchi Goals are established bottom up and achieved top down. We must establish goals at the bottom to support the goals of the Department of Human Services, city of Chicago and to be achieved top down of providing Meaningful, on the job training for clients that will lead to, meaningful employment, and restoring the city's non-tax, paying vacant homes, which are a source of crime such as murders and shooting.

We must present the right picture to investors and lenders, who we plan to be Doctors and professional lenders and investors as long as they are in our target market, geographical area, since they are used to financing homes for upwards of $200,000 and there are many of these in our targeted area that meet that Criteria, but the community has been stigmatized by Zillow Trulia and Red Fin as Danger zones. We must convince investors that there is a good opportunity in the low end of the market and that people will purchase homes in these areas, keep them up and pay their mortgage.

## Chapter-10: The Business Plan

The Structure
Co Op Community Development LLC
A Delaware LLC formed in November 2016
It's Chicago, Illinois      60628 which is in the Roseland community
The Ownership
Eddie Franklin

The Goals and Objectives
   The goal of our company is to build our own real estate construction and real estate services company, by rehabbing homes in the inner-city, by on the job training individuals from the Welfare to Work Program in the skills needed to rehab homes, carpentry, electrical, plumbing, siding, roofing, painting, dry walling, glazing, flooring, job supervision under real services. We will train people on the job in real estate management, leasing and evictions, collection of rent , screening of tenants, and maintenance, and all the while maintaining our profits margins of at least 50 % FIFTY PER CENT.

The product
   The product will be real estate classified as residential units up to 4, the mix of the real estate will be 10% wholesaling, 10% buy and hold, 10% lease option.
 Flipping houses is a JOB where you WORK to find a house WORK to rehab it and WORK to find a buyer to make a one-time profit, and then you WORK to find

another and so on. Lease Option to Own is a BUSINESS, where you find a home rehab it and lease it to someone who has money, but needs to repair their credit. By leasing to them you help stabilize a community, and create streams of income that are residual, providing month income over the term of the option period that is usually 4 years, and sizable cash out at the end of the term, but lease option allows you to use the value of the property to create other lease options through mortgaging the property and pulling equity out from the start. This allows you to have several streams income, even with little or no WORK it provides a monthly income stream for each one, and 70% of the properties will be fix and resale.

The Target Market for Purchasing Homes

The target will be HUD foreclosures and properties from www.myhousedeals.com and private wholesalers' sites and bank owned REOs in the Englewood and Roseland areas primarily, other communities on the South and West sides of the city of Chicago, and properties gained from our websites where we will advertise that we buy house and homes for sale www.coopcommuitydevelopment.com

The Pricing Strategy

Our pricing strategy will find us in the upper part of the Middle of the home buying market up to $150,000 and in the upper part of the low end of the homes from $70,000 up to $150,000. This, of course, depends on the opportunity.

Organizational Theory

Organizational theory is one of Z Theory where the organizational function areas work together in small groups and then present their suggestions and finding to the owners who also operate under the Z Theory.

Ownership Background and Experience

Eddie Franklin, a Retired Management Consultant of Alexander Proudfoot Co, Abbott Laboratories, managing cost reduction and productive programs, Globetrotter Engineering, Chicago Economic Development Corp, consulting to minority businesses. A former Real Estate Broker, the Owner of Accurate Materials and
Construction Company, A Sewer, Water Main Drainage and Plumbing Company and a former superintendent for the Chicago Park District and Chicago Housing Authority for the building trades and a Blogger on the Real Estate Industry. He Is Also Secretary of the Company
Management Structure.
The company will be organized, along functional areas, acquisitions procurement, sales and rehabbing. On internet marketing we expect to have 5% to 10% of our income to come from publishing on YouTube, Monetized blogs, books, and https://www.gofundme.com/2t83qfw and www.patreon.com.

Organizational TimeLine and Location

We plan to acquire our first property to rehab by April 1,of 2018.

Company Assets

Our primary assets are our virtual properties; our domain name blogs, YouTube videos, websites books and soft wares to promote them.

We plan the acquisition and estimated rehab cost is less than 65% of the after-repair value and we get these types of opportunities every week in emails. These lenders require at least 10% this would allow us to borrow up to $135,000 one hundred and thirty five on a property with an after repair of upwards of $200,000 two hundred thousand dollars and there many of these in your communities but our focus will be the under $100,000 one hundred thousand with 3 bed room.

Marketing Plan

The marketing plan is one of the most important pieces of the total plan; the first thing we will do is create a theme "From Welfare to Work with Co Op Community Development LLC "then we will brand it in all of our publishing and advertising.

A. Location Analysis

The locations we have chosen have been stigmatized in the media and on all of the real estate sites Zillow, Red Fin and others as" Hot Zones" meaning these are zones with high shooting and murder rates. It is true that Englewood and Roseland and the Westside have high murder rates, and yet these are communities where hard working and God fearing people live and would purchase a home if it were rehabbed if the price and financing were right. We have to survey these communities using a Cartesian grid of 5 blocks, in which we rate the neighborhood, people standing on corners, liquor stores, Churches, the number of abandoned and boarded up homes on the blocks, and ask people would you purchase a home on this block, if the price and financing were right, etc. This is the criteria that we will use when we find a home for sale before we purchase it, here again, we can use the welfare to work program to use the 20 hours people to do this work on a need basis. These would not be full-time employees. There are good neighborhoods in all these communities. We must find them since the bottom line is that we are in business to make a profit. We must convince our investors and lenders who are mostly white that we have effectively evaluated these neighborhoods for investment possibilities and that they are safe investments.

B.     Pricing Strategy

Our pricing strategy would be low to moderate cost producer for quality and amenities of home we provide in any community we rehab and sale in, while still maintaining our net profit margin of 50%. This will involve aggressive purchasing, cost reduction and productive programs, of which I have over 20 years working experience and consulting for major corporations, institutionalizing cost reduction and productivity programs.

C.     Advertising

Our advertising will be mostly local in the neighborhood where the property is located, using bandit signs flyers, which would market offers to first time home buyers with opportunities for get grants from the Illinois Housing Development Authority (IHDA), Federal Home Loan Bank (FHLB) and local community Banks that would in some cases allow the new home buyer the opportunity to purchase a home with 1 to 5% down or a gift from a family member as down payment. These first time home buyers are also able to get grants of up to the 1 one to 5 five percent A first-time homeowner is someone who has not owned a home in the past 3years. This would allow a person even after a bankruptcy or foreclosure that has a FICA score 580 or more to purchase another home. We would also advertise on local radio, internet radio, and on Facebook, Twitter, and other social media sites. We would market wholesale properties via email using a private server to a list of over 5000 wholesalers in the State of Illinois and advertise properties to the 37,000 real estate brokers in Illinois using this same server. We would also advertise properties to cash buyers who are purchasing in Chicago through the resources provide on www.myhousedeals.com. This is where we could purchase properties or find funding by sending out emails in a closed private system to buyer's sellers and lenders for the Chicagoland or any area nationwide.

D.    Marketing Strategy

Our market strategy would be nationwide and worldwide branding our model "From Welfare to Work with Co Op Community Development," using websites and a squeeze/email capture page, which will include video training, in nationwide marketing campaigns .

We also use www.YouTube.com to make video on our own YouTube channels and get paid for views on our channel from advertising revenues collected by YouTube from ads placed on our video. We will also brand the Chicago Model to over 1 million real estate broker in the United States using a private server by email. We will do this by setting up the program in a monetized blog with Google AdWords and anyone who clicks on this ad on our site will pay up to $4 per click, and we will

share the revenue paid to Google. The pay per click price for a keyword like real estate is about $4 per click; we will share this revenue from Google. We will have full time welfare to work in charge of all our internet based marketing and he or she will be constantly training the 20-hour part-time person to find someone to work with him or her as we grow. This person will be responsible for posting new relevant content to all of our internet marketing sites daily, to Blogs, to Facebook groups, to Twittter webinars and podcast. The 20-hour person will be trained to ping the blog site daily in order to call the Google spider to crawl, the site and get it the first page of google for real estate rehab.

Email marketing and eBooks publishing will be another source of nationwide marketing being marketed on E-Bay and Amazon and as a how to do the book.

Competition Analysis

A. Mad House Deals

No one is making a concerted effort to purchase HUD homes in the areas we are targeting as our market. I, my family and many friends were purchasing HUD home over 40 years ago and you had to visit 20 or so to find one worth investing, but today with the advent of the cell phone with cameras, the Real Estate agent responsible for these homes always had to visit them every week but now they have to take pictures, that are time and date stamped and HUD has become very aggressive winterization program years ago, it was typical of HUD home to find frozen water damage to pipes and toilets. Many of the under $15,000 homes in These, communities that we target only need painting and minor repairs and advertising them back to public who already live in the neighborhood. Here is the site https://www.hudhomestore.com/Home/Index.aspx.

B. Mom and Pop Rehabbers

Mom and pop rehabbers are mostly Hispanic who only want to have a few homes to rent or sell to relatives.

C. Most organizations Associated with County Land Bank

Authority don't have the theory or organizational ability or experience to be competitors and are only interested in gaining grant money from the state and have no program for end buyers and first time home buyers.

SWOT Analysis

Strength/Weakness/Opportunities
1. Strength
The strength of the organization lies in the coalition that we have built, with nonprofits in the field of training, and nonprofits in the field working within the prison system to facilitate the reentry of patrons to main society, and the commitment of men and women who care and have years of experience in doing what they do.

2. Weakness
The weakness is the fact that we are a new company and the innovative approach to the real estate construction and management is unprecedented at the scale we envision. We must educate America on this approach.

3. Opportunities
 The opportunity is that the real estate market has been recovering for the past 18 months and it is predicted to be on the edge of the record recovery of the which happened in the first quarter of 2006.
   Real estate plays an integral role in the U.S. economy. Residential real estate provides housing for families. It's often the greatest source of wealth and savings for many of them. Commercial real estate, which includes apartment buildings, creates spaces for jobs in retail, offices and manufacturing. Real estate income provides a source of revenue for millions.

In 2015, real estate construction contributed $990 billion to the nation's economic output.

That's 6% of U.S. Gross Domestic Product (GDP). That's getting closer to its peak of $1.195 trillion in 2006. At that time, it was a hefty 8.9% component of GDP. Real estate construction is labor intensive. That's why a drop-in housing construction was a big contribution to the recession's high unemployment rate.

New construction is the only part of real estate that's measured by GDP. It affects many other areas of economic well-being that aren't measured as well. For example, a decline in real estate sales eventually leads to a decline in real estate prices. That lowers the value of all homes, whether owners are actively selling it or not. It reduces the number of home equity loans available to owners. They will cut back on consumer spending.

And with the return of reserve requirement for banks to some closer to Glass Stegall and the repeal or the amending of Dodd Frank which both parties support. The release of $910,000,000,000 billion dollars for lending on FHA loans, almost a trillion dollars.

Staffing

The only staff will be the owner and other will be hired as need from the Welfare to Work Program or TANF Temporary Assistance to Needy Families. They will be brought as need demands and some will be evaluated and hired as permanent employees.

Strategy Plan for Company Owners

1. Institutionalization

The owners will grow in the knowledge of the community they serve and understanding of the right neighborhood in a community that they can safely purchase and rehab homes in and generate a profit and maintain our profit margin of a minimum of 50% by having written surveys of the neighborhoods using a Cartesian grid format and rating the blocks, so no one owner is required to make a decision on where to purchase.

2. Cross Training

The owner and managers also will be crossed trained as well as the staff to perform all the duties required for their function.

3. Written Procedures

Written procedure will be developed as to every key function of the business and systems will be developed to support those function so no one employee or owner will ever become indispensable to the operation of the company.

4. Succession Plan

Over years I have seen so many multimillion dollar minority construction companies fail because they did not have a succession plan, Archway Steel Company, Glen Harriston Archway Steel Company has thousands of unclaimed dollars with no one to claim them, World Plumbing Company. We will develop a plan of succession for our heirs or a designated successor.

## Cash Flow Projections

Roseland is up 25% over the Last 3 months with the price of a 3 bedroom going from $100,000 to $125,000, form Trulia figures based on 5% appreciation per year and a 50% increase per year in number of homes sold.

### Pro Forma Cash Flow Statement from April, 1, 2018 thru December 31, 2018

|  | April | May | June | July | Aug | Sep | Oct | Nov | Dec | Total |
|---|---|---|---|---|---|---|---|---|---|---|
| Homes | 2 | 6 | 9 | 8 | 8 | 8 | 8 | 8 | 3 | 60 |
| Rev | $199.5K | $598.5K | $897K | $798K | $798K | $798K | $798K | $798K | $299K | |
| Per Month | $99.75K | $299.25K | $448.5K | $399K | $399K | $399K | $399K | $399K | $99.5K | |

Cash Flow
Total homes Sold 60
Average Selling Price $99,750
Total Revenue $5,985,000/2=$2,992,500 Profit

# Pro Forma Cash Flow Statement 5 Year Plan

| Year | Rose land | Engle wood | Total Areas | Aver | Home | Rev | 50% Profit |
|------|-----------|------------|-------------|------|------|-----|------------|
| 1 | $125,000 | $74,500 | $199,500 | $99,750 | 60 | $5,985,000 | $2,992,500 |
| 2 | $131,250 | $79,170 | $210,420 | $105,200 | 90 | $9,468,000 | $4,734,000 |
| 3 | $137,818 | $83,128 | $214,378 | $107,189 | 135 | $14,470,515 | $7,235,258 |
| 4 | $144,703 | $87,248 | $231,951 | $115,975 | 203 | $23,543,026 | $11,771,513 |
| 5 | $151,938 | $91,649 | $243,587 | $121,794 | 304 | $37,025,376 | $18,512,688 |

Total homes 792

Total profits $45,245,959

Note after 5 years we will expand into the cities of Gary, In, Atlanta, GA, New Orleans, LA and Dallas TX

## The projections below are for Chicago, Illinois figures based on 3% appreciation

| Yr. | Rose land | Engle wood | Total Areas | Aver | Homes | Rev | 50% Profit |
|-----|-----------|------------|-------------|------|-------|-----|------------|
| 6 | $156,496 | $94,389 | $250,894 | $125,447 | 456 | $57,203,832 | $28,601.196 |
| 7 | $161,191 | $97,230 | $258,421 | $129,211 | 684 | $88,380,324 | $44,190,162 |
| 8 | $166,027 | $100,147 | $266,174 | $133,087 | 1026 | $136,547,262 | $68,273,631 |
| 9 | $171,008 | $103,152 | $274,160 | $137,080 | 1534 | $210,966,120 | $105,483,060 |
| 10 | $176,138 | $106,246 | $282,384 | $141,192 | 2309 | $326,012,328 | $163,006,164 |
| 11 | $181,422 | $109,434 | $290,856 | $145,428 | 3463 | $503,617,164 | $251,808,582 |
| 12 | $186,865 | $112,717 | $299,582 | $149,791 | 5195 | $778,164,245 | $389,082,123 |
| 13 | $192,471 | $116,098 | $308,569 | $154,285 | 7793 | $1,202,343,005 | $601,171,503 |
| 14 | $198 | $119,5 | $317, | $158, | 11,6 | $1,857,72 | $928,864, |

| | ,244 | 87 | 831 | 916 | 90 | 0,040 | 020 |
|---|---|---|---|---|---|---|---|
| 15 | $204 ,191 | $123,1 68 | $327, 359 | $163, 680 | 17,5 35 | $2,870,12 8,800 | $1,435,06 4,400 |

Total Home Rehabbed 51,001
Profits $4,716,417,140

## We Make Our Profit when We Buy

These figure represent purchasing homes for less than 20% of after repair value and homes with less than 30% of repair cost to after repair value. This would be purchasing home in Roseland for less than $25,000, we would consider paying up to $30,000 since the values are currently rising, at 25% over the last 3 months and buying in Englewood for less the $15,000. The figures for repair cost will remain as stated above.

We are open to investors investing with us, for more information call Eddie L. Franklin 630 380 4297.

www.ingramcontent.com/pod-product-compliance
Lightning Source LLC
Chambersburg PA
CBHW071239220526
45468CB00002B/926